# capricornucopia
# (the dream of the goats)

*poems by*

# paulA neves

*Finishing Line Press*
Georgetown, Kentucky

# capricornucopia
# (the dream of the goats)

*for Setinha*

Copyright © 2018 by paulA neves
ISBN 978-1-63534-451-6 First Edition
All rights reserved under International and Pan-American Copyright Conventions. No part of this book may be reproduced in any manner whatsoever without written permission from the publisher, except in the case of brief quotations embodied in critical articles and reviews.

## ACKNOWLEDGMENTS

The following poems have appeared, sometimes in different forms, in the following publications:

This Isn't Angola or Mozambique (*O Preto*) (*Newest Americans*, 2018)
Capricornucopia (*Fiolet and Wing, An Anthology of Domestic Fabulist Poetry*, edited by Stacey Balkun and Catherine Moore, 2017).
Offerings Ofensas (*The Acentos Review,* 2017).
Work (*The Abuela Stories Project*, edited by Peggy Robles-Alvarado, 2016).
Paralelos (*InterDISCIPLINARY Journal of Portuguese Diaspora Studies*, 2015).
11th Birthday, The (Almost) Married Guide to Tourist Traps, Train to Lisbon (*Writers of the Portuguese Diaspora in the United States and Canada*, edited by Luis Gonçalves and Carlo Matos, Boa Vista Press, 2015).
Nap (Rocky Mtns—Come Again!) (*Pilgrimage Magazine*, edited by Juan Morales, Colorado State University-Pueblo, 2015).
Utah 1 (*Luna Luna Magazine*, 2015).
Transcript (*Between Mountain*, edited by Marte Danielsen Jølbo and Nick Kline, Norway, 2012).


Publisher: Leah Maines
Editor: Christen Kincaid
Cover Art: paulA neves
Author Photo: Devyn N. Nunez & Shelly Edelman
Cover Design: Elizabeth Maines McCleavy


Printed in the USA on acid-free paper.
Order online: www.finishinglinepress.com
also available on amazon.com

Author inquiries and mail orders:
Finishing Line Press
P. O. Box 1626
Georgetown, Kentucky 40324
U. S. A.

# Table of Contents

Graciete .................................................................................................... 1

Lazarus Squirms ..................................................................................... 2

This Isn't Angola or Mozambique (O Preto) ................................... 4

Passing a Fibroid at an Off-Broadway Production of *Medea* ........ 5

Capricornucopia (The Dream of the Goats) .................................... 6

Casino Figueira da Foz ......................................................................... 8

11th Birthday ......................................................................................... 9

Transcript .............................................................................................. 11

America Un-admitted ......................................................................... 14

The (Almost) Married Couple's Guide to Tourist Traps .............. 15

Nap (Rocky Mtns—Come Again!) .................................................. 16

Ma Watched Birds from Her Hospital Blinds (Bird Slants) ........ 17

Pearl River ............................................................................................. 18

Paralelos ................................................................................................ 19

The Catholic and the Mormon Who Met at Mardi Gras ............ 20

Train to Lisbon .................................................................................... 21

Utah 1 .................................................................................................... 22

Work ...................................................................................................... 23

Annapolis .............................................................................................. 24

Offerings Ofensas ................................................................................ 25

Summer Spent ..................................................................................... 26

Caldeirada ............................................................................................ 28

Math and English Word Problem (3/4 sleeve blouse) ................. 30

Living Dangerously ............................................................................ 32

**Graciete**

she taught me to play
potato skins

like a strop,
the peels eye-lid thin—

because why should flesh
suffer

when meat matters most

in a linoleum kitchen
in a newark dim

pulaski st. building?
the corner church

is st. casimir's problem
not hers,

so why should she light
a candle for fatima

be her own burden

when water beats
in the sink

sluices the chicken's cold skin
with abandon?

I will listen to her
just once more

while she cradles the blade
in one hand

insisting that I
unravel.

## Lazarus Squirms

> *and life tells me to embrace what is perishable*
> *rather than choosing the record of what was.* —Rachel Hadas

the hospital solstice      in april
delivered her      home

                new and pain clean

through each generation    each
peeled    layer    of        mask and gauze

pinched from drawers
        bright    bloodless      rooms

where    layers have use
        where    walls        remember

that she rested

through june's drawn-    blind
attachment        to may,

july's            straggler magnolias,
august's curled        sycamore      leaves,

too early    too late      for all
hallow's eve.      she rested and rose

to try legs she called    washed up        eels
turned        back into salt

denied the current    of
sashay and faith

proper balance    on woman—    or ungain-ly
hips        cradle of no more

betrayals    from which      she rises
now        on others' time,

their bird bones stronger,
amphibian apologies    to flight

rescinded but they      retract their wings—
dragons not saints    they can    rise

on their own				why don't they?!
their bodies too

will leave them	in		emergency
berths			where she

plays solataire with lazarus
names the old years,			dogs	she put down,

asks	where's jesus	now
that his mother's stopped cooking

reminisces about birth				—lazarus squirms,

turns on the TV

### This Isn't Angola or Mozambique (O Preto)
*—after Carrie Mae Weems' I Looked and Looked to See What So Terrified You*

I looked and looked to see what would work.
I laughed in the vanity, eyes lined with kohl.

Caveira I was with night years for eyes, you at 2
could not tell mother from skull on the cover of the Times—

Lord, at 19, with you, I felt as old as that Lucy
delivered by the mailman who, luckily, was black,

perfect timing because you wouldn't eat your soup.
*O Preto will get you! O Preto!* "No, I eat, I eat!"—

as I collected the mail for the Americans upstairs.
You never saw him on the stoop, but thank God you knew

just from his being that you'd better believe.
My bruxa eyes made you clean only half of your bowl.

Try me again. No child of mine will make others accuse
me of neglect. *This isn't Angola or Mozambique.*

## Passing a Fibroid at an Off-Broadway Production of *Medea*

intermission at the ny theater workshop
a bathroom line as long as gut
but I was impatient and pushed through—
*hey lady, what the fuck?*

inside, my jeans barely down—
surprise! months after the procedure
that cut off blood to the *equivalent* of 12 weeks' growth
i think of furtive teenagers in high school stalls.

but we're not like them, are we, medea?
we're tempered women—though I'm no queen.
still, you'd appreciate the irony
when what is neither past nor promise slides out of you—

no medium for love or vengeance or remorse
no ears, eyes, limbs or perfect toes
just a lump of undifferentiated muscle cells
from a hereditary broth.

*when you have children someday…*
our foremothers and the gods pronounced.
you were not meant to, observes the audience
as if, for each of us, that were enough.

## Capricornucopia (The Dream of the Goats)

Goats appeared at the door,
asking to eat the house from inside out.
It was Christmas, so we let them enter.
The drink-laden guests parted.

Sure footed on the walnut-inlaid parquet,
the beasts made for the manger first,
ate the fake hay with unbridled relish.

The billygoat then eyed the end tables
my girlfriends and I had saved from curbs
and I had carried on my back
to whatever places we were calling home.

All the females followed billyboy's suit—
whatever they're called, *girlygoats*?
I know what they are but regardless

everyone looked at me as if the goats
could see through walls—
an insight out of Freud or Foucault.
My new girlfriend looked pissed.

The goats made for the sofa.
"Who are they to you?" My girlfriend insisted.
Stuffing fell about us like snow.

The billygoat toppled the tree.
Blown glass ornaments blew everywhere.
Some shattered. Some dangled
from his horns like disco earrings.

"Androgyny went out in the 80's,
when you were still young,"
I heard at my ear.

I hoped it was the voice of the devil
I didn't know—a future lover perhaps,
her flutes as piercing, her heart as cloven
as any Pan I could ask for (and have).

But it was only my mother,
who whispered, "Did you ever
turn on the oven?"
Then added, "You're starting to get whiskers,

just like them."
Tender, the words went through me like a horn.

Mercifully, someone shouted, "They're headed for the table!"
And so the goats were. Like midnight buffet tourists,
they charged the sweetmeats, the Mouton Cadet,
the *chanfana*\* like grandma used to make.

"Cannibalism. At Christmas no less,"
a faceless relative
tsk tsk'ed.

Let them.
Let them be goats.
Let them eat everything—

                                          even the bones.

---

\* Traditional Portuguese goat or mutton dish oven-stewed in wine.

## Casino Figueira da Foz

It doesn't translate. Figueira da Foz:
*Fig tree at the mouth of the river,* she'd tell co-workers,
whether fellow Portuguese or mildly disinterested Americans.

*Doesn't it mean estuary of the fig tree?* I contested—
That brackish place where a half-strung kid with a guitar
sang fados about a lightmaker.

*Lighting technician* she corrects me silently from the employee ID card
next to the passport, Q-tips and other heirlooms in the drawer,
the photo taken the year or two before our trip

when she still sat at lathes and shaped quartz bulbs
like those that pulsed outside the casino's walls.
*Impressive,* she said, as any ramparts on our sightseers route.

Street pilgrims painted faces, traded fortunes, juggled fires,
painted portraits for cêntimos on the dollar.
A young man who braided plaits looked a little out of it

among the Vandals, Suevi, Visigoths.
He knitted a tired little girl's locks
with a patience and practiced art

she had no time for when I was the daughter
of the fishermen who mended nets
on postcards of the beach in the afternoons.

I did not mention this while she played roulette.

## 11th Birthday

They are all here.
Neighbors, cousins, mother's co-workers,
primped in polyester on the plastic-covered couch,
their children with their hands on everything
(*badly educated* as Ma would say—
except on special occasions).

To impress them, on my 11th birthday
I sit at the piano, the one Ma bought,
after two months of Saturday shifts,
from Maria Marques, because her daughter, Diana,
after just one year of learning herself,
started giving lessons and outgrew it.

*Va la,* go on, play us something understandable,
they urge, instead of all this jangling.
Then tell your sticky-handed brats to leave, I think,
when Diana, already a lady at 12, takes her place
beside me on the bench, turns to the last page,
and starts the count, quieting them instantly.

Surprise! I clank through my own "Happy Birthday."
Diana hums to keep the beat—futilely,
as everyone sings it in their keys.

How long this lasts I'll never remember.
Meanwhile,

the food waits on the table we never use:
Wonder Bread, Shop Rite cola,
yellow butter crème cake from Coutinho's
decorated in cursive thin as veins
(from which those little fingersmiths
have already swiped the 'day').

Apart from this there are the staples:
potatoes, rice, the deep fried cod fritters
they all call *balls*, which, if I look
at Diana now, would make me titter—
understanding, as I am,
how concerned they all are with *appearances*.

So, instead, I hit a wrong F sharp on purpose
and offer it to Diana (whose conducting never wavers)

as small revenge for playing along with our mothers,
who wouldn't want us to misrepresent
why at other people's houses we get the stare of death
if we dare to entertain a "yes"
when we are offered
anything.

**Transcript**

you remember her face like a postcard from the sea:
the faded blue, the drifting edges,
the dun background, stiff seagull feathers.

\*

luminescence means
you could take for granted again
the taste of pennies on your own tongue.

\*

unpaired umbrellas still take up twice their space
on this narrow strip of Broadway.
they crowd me out. i'm almost 42.

\*

in the autumn
he disappeared down the storm cellar hatch.
the smell of sleep has always haunted us—

\*

the elevator opens into the apartment
and the lines that vanish in all of us
are dormant seeds in window boxes:

\*

the woman who was once your mother's age
when secret police asked what she had to offer

should not have stayed in country
to set old smoke alight

should not have insisted
with eyes of polished copper

\*

how the Maya must have sacrificed their hearts;
a new moon on the bone of winter night.

\*

he emerged with gallons of new wine.
though, like the wedding jugs at Cana,
they never seemed to run out.

\*

childhood nights the floor is ceiling
and overhead green-yellow bulb
out of a reproduction of the *Night Cafe*

is so bright it might blind
if not that the throat closes so fast
it automatically shuts the eyes.

\*

reflection reveals we are only carbon deep,
no body to eclipse the space of what's left,
to fill the four corners of each year with a room.

\*

i'll leave my longing and your house alone.
he planted a kitchen garden in the spring.

\*

when you close your eyes, will you still see
through the crosshatch of shroud

the small beauty mark, wine-dark mole
in the center of the eyelid

covering the sailor's eye
i inherited from you?

\*

this shiny-eyed sadness is only a reminder.
outside, the summer ache of spiders spins the air.

\*

over friendly drinks she says
*timing is everything,*

and I reply
*fractals*

the way some people say
*bullshit*

like it was
*liminal*

\*

could you give me something to eat? he says
i'm so hungry
his windbreaker streaked by mid November
his cap a half-pulled cork

and i am tempted to respond *sir, we are all hungry,*
but of course I don't,
tuck my guilt under my arm,
my mouth caked dry for lunch.

**America Un-admitted**

That this one's face is half new moon full
Mother's milk and father's coal tar
Chinese opera and Mardi Gras

Guilded dust on dead sister's dresser
Ace of clubs dogged
In brother's drowned rucksack

An overpass where the blood burned
Into the earth who forgives…again
Big sky sun where white is not

Possum wisdom the neighbor shot
With amphetamine glint
In the noon dark sun

That this one's face is not
Smoke and mirror just crème cacao
Blood black angel in the snow

Warsaw ghetto where grandfathered stars
Were only half seen in the half light
So the stars might have forgot

That this is Newark and Standing Rock
Where Jesus lookalikes at JFK
Learn customs out of 1938

And this one's face has seen Ra
This one's face has been crow
This one's face

And this one's face
Is this one's face
You know

## The (Almost) Married Couple's Guide to Tourist Traps

In Lamanai we learned how the Maya might have sacrificed their hearts
while we, lapsed vegetarians, ate local spiced sweetmeats ourselves

to read the future in splayed seagull carcasses along the Great Salt Lake
so that New Orleans Indians would last until the next apocalypse

in that Baja town where trannies pass for wives until the real thing comes along
while we, women ourselves, played possum for the Day of the Dead

so that west of Oranjestad you could swim with fishes in the Mouth of Hell
and I could watch you, with something halfway between envy and regret

until Oporto offered up a river of English wines—
so we could toast our never staying long enough in one place.

**Nap (Rocky Mtns—Come Again!)**

\*

you're still deciding what to dream
when the last rag and bone man
hawks his wares down Ferry St.

\*

outside the oiled window shades,
sparrows, catbirds, whatever

calls you from the sycamores
(that twist like your grandparents' hands)

throw shadows like exclamations
across the crocheted bedspread.

\*

somehow your mother never sleeps
with dishes waiting in the sink.

her waking looks like, you guess,
the burning hills of Buçaco forest

that she talked about at Sunday dinner once—
how every summer some idiot tourist threw a match,

to end it.

\*

your father ate stewed rabbit and didn't hear
the details she borrowed about the apocalypse

from cousins and visinhos* after church.

v.
you never sleep again yourself,
whole nights waiting for him to come home,

burning just to catch a glimpse
of bird shaped water pistols

or key fobs declaring, "Rocky Mtns—Come Again!"—
whatever presents he'd pinched from Port Elizabeth and Newark

lying on the kitchen table at dawn.

---

\* Neighbors

**Ma Watched Birds from Her Hospital Blinds (Bird Slants)**

another day
wrens were respite or regret

unending fable
that skin sheds

grief molts
we all take the bait

that what is underfoot
beneath the spinal birch

small birds
will not make us f(l)inch

red heralds
stillborn in the throat

will re-emerge
(sp)arrow taut

bone and sinew snapped
like an afterthought

hours pared
to their mitochondrial light

give birth: *dar a luz*\*
is how we hedge our bets

how our mother tongue
forgets the word for *missed*

how we explain
away the window's filth

why doctors entertain
where Daedalus got the wax

forgetting the sun
broken on our backs.

---

\* Literally, "give to the light."

**Pearl River**
    *—after Ezra Pound*

When I wore my favorite jeans for you for the first time
I stood in the street outside the Pearl River nervously waiting.
You emerged from the gray coats and umbrellas of that November's rain,
all scarlet scarf and reclaimed thrift store go-go boots.
And we went inside to shop for a life we were sure we'd have.
The store was thriving kitsch then. You bought me a tea ball
from a bin of many, and mentioned how hot
the cheap red dresses would look on me:
"You're tiny enough to wear one," you said. Tiny.
A word I'd always hated until you.

At 37 I'd stopped scowling.
I wanted my tomboy tees and unmatched silverware
to mingle with yours
forever and forever and forever.
Why should I buy anything more?

At 41 you said it's over.
You walked me down Broadway as far as my World Trade Center stop
and kept going towards Brooklyn.
And you have been gone 15 months.
My Walmart boots make sorrowful noise when I walk.

You didn't look back when you went on.
The Pearl River is gone now. The window displays are all H&M,
the cheap dresses gone—lost to street vendors, too many to choose from!
The leaves fall late this autumn, in wind and sleety rain.
Unpaired umbrellas still take up twice their space
on this narrow strip of Broadway;
they crowd me out.
                I'm almost 42.

**Paralelos**

While I stand with a coffee outside the 7-Eleven in Westchester, PA,
the day I introduced you to the eucalyptus, the curious looks,
the diesel *carrinhas* stirring up the dust
is only a day.

While I stand outside the 7-Eleven, good morning Pennsylvanians
parade Americana, and we are having our *sesta* (not *siesta*, that's Spain),
and wide awake, I am slinking towards you, on hands and knees,
in my grandfather's widower's bed

because we have the house to ourselves,
because he lies dying in a convalescent casa in Pedreira, Anadia,
and I breath the idea in your ear afterwards, as our bodies relax,
that we should rise the way he no longer can,

walk the *kilometros* of gravel and *paralelos* in our flip flops to visit him,
because you always wanted to go to Fátima, and this was,
as we stare at the rosary hung heart-shaped above the headboard and laugh,
as close as we would get

to the cold *fininhos* afterwards,
to the curious look the barmaid gave us
when we tipped her too much, two bedraggled *Americanas*,
each standing outside convenience stores somewhere.

## The Catholic and the Mormon Who Met at Mardi Gras

I'm on a mission chasing you, former chaser,
back to the Big Easy where our masquerade began.
There, you showed me one Fat Tuesday was no baser
than the Monday to Sunday drag of those who pretend
protection with the gris-gris bits of home to work to bed,
scheduled sex, meals, workouts, movies in between:
Marriage. Some call that love, better than the head
space we got into on Ecstasy, when you confessed
you didn't need much (just a smile) to get undressed,
make many children for the afterlife with me.
As if! Ah, silly girl, parthenogenesis is Mary's deal,
and her son simply a guy in a long dress,
and, despite appearances, I'm not the boy of my father's eye—
just a girl who wants to find you again and proselytize.

**Train to Lisbon**

We took a train down the Portuguese coast and got drunk
on the wine and pastries we carefully packed in the trunk
we hoisted everywhere on our two-week Silver Coast junk-
et; the small bottles of *tinto* and the *pasteis* eased our post-argument funk.

We stopped sulking long enough to ease the wine and pastries from the trunk,
relieved, after missing the express and waiting for hours in a park in Cacém;
the small bottles of *red* and the *sweets* eased our post-argument funk
better than the stale bread we'd bought fresh in Sintra the previous day.

We waited sullenly for hours in that park in Cacém.
"That's not how it happened!" I hear you object
because we'd found Byron, not bread, in Sintra the previous day.
But lyrics aren't much concerned with the facts.

"That's not how it happened!" one always objects,
and sustenance is one of the fictions of our days.
Besides, lyrics aren't much concerned with the facts;
so this is what I mean put a different way:

Bread is just one of the fictions of that day,
as was that cumbersome love, I mean, trunk, and the sweet drunken talk.
So this is what I mean put a different way:
When the train got to Lisbon, I walked.

**Utah 1**

Those we've forgotten have faces
of faded blues, drifting edges,
dun backgrounds, Indian feathers.

On the back of these post cards
there are always a few well-scripted words:
*Saltaire's carousel rings out its portents.*
Random sparks in the kerosene air.

We wander the wreck of the lake, the pavilion, the flats.
*Your people swam in the Great Salt Lake*—I state the obvious.
Mine tried to pass at feast tables of roast suckling pig,
became clean enough to earn Salazar's blessing.

It takes generations to invent a new West.
Seagull carcasses jewel every salted coast.

No Chelsea margarita can make us forget this.

**Work**

Ordered, making change at Burger King,
I didn't cop to knowing "who"
when high school classmates, taunting, ordered fries
again and again, and asked,

"Who's that old bat in the window?
She know you?"

How could she know me and
how could I know
how much plate-glass her palm-framed face
had already looked through?

"Not all work is work," she always said,
"Take it from me"—

who traveled 3000 miles
and one rush hour Broad Street intersection
to verify the gravitas of mopping, wiping or simply waiting
had not been lost on me.

Later at home she said, "You pretended not to know me,
but I know you, better than you think."
But what I thought was,
*God, I'll be a journeywoman, just like you—*

always polishing surfaces,
hoping to find what's underneath.

## Annapolis

That afternoon, the bosses drove us to downtown Annapolis,
promised lobster at that top notch joint the locals all love.

Their assistant at the plant said it was, "no expenses spared,"
the kind of thing where they "wheeled and dealed all the big cats." She winked.

But you are just a mere "technician," as you noted in the morning interview.
Why bother bringing me, your first and only daughter

to your first and only interview in 30 years
if you won't listen to what I tell you?

 "What I think my mother means,"
I glanced at you across the table so that you'd get the hint,

"Is that she has worked enough with quartz technology
to know the difference between all your lamps."

I'll just take 10% like an agent, I thought, amused,
instead of just the Amtrak ride.

At lunch, Bob and Carl, the brother-bosses who headed
The Specialized Lighting Corporation, strained for chit chat

over their cheesesteaks and crab bisque.
My mother, country girl at heart, didn't say much

over her chicken sandwich. Neither did I, the vegetarian,
over a salad of arugula and pignoli nuts.

**Offerings Ofensas**
      *—after an ad in the Lisbon Metro recalling PIDE's victims*

for more than a braid of a daughter's hair
or a son's milk teeth wrapped in chita
the priest-professor told you to believe

so you believed
in economies of ofertas
you believed in Fátima and fadistas

who sang of sailors and their strong sea
legs, taking them anywhere but Tarrafal
far from your honeyed wax heart

far from the woman like your mother
who carried your perfeito coração
hoping the gulls would eat from her hand

hoping just one would have come
instead of PIDE to ask
what she had to offer

if she believed in her own ofensas
*perdoai as nossas…ai Senhor*
if she believed her feet were anchors

or there but for the grace of God
pillars of a house
where they'd set old smoke on fire

again and again insisting
with eyes the brass of chalices
that she shouldn't have

**Summer Spent**

As you latch the gate on New York Ave.,
the haze over Newark holds you close,

as close to the city as her last dream.
The metal clasp rings like Sunday,

reminds you of all the other covenants,
the sidewalk's simple fractured facts:

this is where the old mis-step,
bloodied their hands and broke their hips;

this is where you saved a stray cat
that now traps itself nightly in hedge or garage.

This morning, as usual, your blouse
whispers against your back and breasts,

but with assignments in purse and briefcase,
you take a moment to let the day stick,

glance at Mr., Mrs. and Jr's front stoop
where, strangely, this early, Jr. is dressed

in shirtsleeves and slacks,
as if for Fatima's first mass,

bouncing a basketball as if it were Prime.
But what does he know about sweat.

It is only Monday.
Closer to Tuesday, when the day is spent

and the haze over Newark
mocks beautiful West,

you will visit and revisit your old mother
at the house where you prayed and she builds and rebuilds

from the soft cartilage of your newborn skull
the cornices and keystones of her broken knees and heart,

varicosed like the sycamore roots
that upended the sidewalk

under the arbor where the grapes hang and fall,
staining the memory of all of your others.

You imagine she will greet you at the door
in a familiar house dress

behind which her breasts settle like dusk.
Instead, she greets you in the kitchen like dawn

with the old yellow counters of recurrence,
and, prescribing penance

for the damp armpits of your ruined blouse,
boils fish, potatoes and garden kale

with an efficiency that belies
her own natural faults.

## Caldeirada

Peel the potatoes, cut into chunks and put in olive oiled water.
Chop in big rough pieces. 1 big tomato.
Buy *lulas* at *Seabra's*. Ask them to clean them. Ask if they'll chop them up for *caldeirada*. If not, chop them yourself, *Tu nao es handicap!*
Chop the *lulas* in pieces, including the legs. No, don't chop the *legs* in pieces, just chop them off and use them. I remember Bob Burke's face when I stuff the legs in the *lulas* and took for lunch to work one time. Is not hamburger helper that's for sure!
Put in water with the pieces of potato and tomato. I bought 2 *lulas*.
Turn stove on high to boil. Electric stove, not so good, but when you don't have a dog,
hunt with a cat.
Use monkfish pieces.
Red snapper pieces.
Pollock pieces. *Que?* What do you mean like *Jack-son Pollock?* Pay attention. *Tas-me ouvir?*
Carrots. Scrape-peel. Chop *e põe na agua* to boil along with the *lulas*. That go in soon, not yet.
Potatoes and tomatoes.
Spanish or yellow onion. Because there's no Portuguese onion ah ha ha. Chop roughly *(what else is new?)* and put in with the other boiling stuff.
O' my god. Is getting so hot in here. Is like climate change.
Bay leaf. Put it in.
Paprika. Sprinkle some in.
Oregano. Do the same.
Garlic or garlic salt. Whatever. What do you think?
Parsley. Of course it's fresh. From the *quintal*. Put it in. But not til the end.
Green pepper. Chop it and throw it. *Wha-?? Did I say against the wall?* How old are you anyway? You getting on my nerves, kid!
Turmeric or saffron for color. Just a *pouquito*. It's expensive you know. I don't care if Emeril says they're not the same thing. He's only half Portuguese.
Wash the salt off the fish chunks and throw in the ones that are, you know, "harder" first. Look, the fish are all in the water again! Only they're dead this time.
Cover pot and let it all boil. Don't aggravate me. It's done when it's done.
When it's almost done, pull apart watercress and throw it in. Until it's done.
O' and a little white wine. I know you like to boozy. You don't get that from my side!
Remember:
Use flouring potatoes.
Use summer tomatoes. Or tomato paste.
You can use other greens, not just watercress.
Of course you salt the water. But if you don't wash the salt off the fish and put in a lotta salt, it'll burn like acid, kid.

I don't like pepper but do what you want.

Now get out of my kitchen.

## Math and English Word Problem (3/4 quarter sleeve blouse)

One eye sees night
As black as my irises
The other sees names
Above mispronounced faces

Lips aslant
Skin slack as defeat
Hospital sheet grayed
By constant hands

3/4 quarter sleeve blouse
Worn for the factory office
Dried stain on the cuff
Our shared AB+

Black running shoes
Atlantic teal accents
At the end of the stretcher
Archipelagoes lost

At the end of the stretcher
The physician mouths gone
In 10 or 12 syllables
Easy enough math

In 10 or 12 sentences
Easy enough life
In 10 or 12 decades
We'll all be on Mars.

But could someone repeat
That the soles are unworn
Before the variables come:
DNI. DNR.

Acronyms meaning
I thought there'd be more
My brother and I are
Grayed like old times

Our father, undone
Our mother
Three decades on
The three of us are

The two of us again
Ask the doctor are you sure?
Nod. Say thank you.
Go on.

**Living Dangerously**

Yes, it's true.
I chase an aspirin or antibiotic
with a martini, or a few,
when it's open bar at a party
so as not to be rude
but mostly ungrateful for the pleasure
of the three swollen olives
at the end.

I cannot lie.
I have picked up many noodles
slipped from the fork
onto the weeks' unwashed linoleum
before I could check if they were al dente enough
and bit them then or threw them back
or ate them standing
if they were perfect.

I acknowledge it.
I have tried on all the size 7 ½ shoes
and some others besides
on many reputable racks
and walked around barefoot in between
on soggy winter carpeting
because I liked even the hint of unbroken leather insoles
against my unwashed skin.

I have never been the type
to keep my hands away from nose or mouth
when walking crowded hallways in public
and never pushed the long bars of stairway exit doors
with my covered elbows
so that contact with others' particles
would be virtually
impossible.

When I'm feeling dangerous
I microwave my lunch in reused
plastic wanton soup containers
or sometimes even in the styrofoam of the steamed vegetable special
so that the thin, invisible film of released fumes
along with the "negligible" microwaves
will inoculate me a little at a time
from the inevitable.

**PaulA neves** is native of the Ironbound section of Newark, NJ, a working class, immigrant neighborhood that has given voice to many artists. It is also, like many such places in America, quickly gentrifying.

Wanting to be either an artist or a writer at an early age and choosing writing as the more "practical" of the two, neves has published in *Newest Americans, The Acentos Review, Cleaver Magazine, The Abuela Stories Project, Queen Mob's Teahouse, Writers of the Portuguese Diaspora, Quiddity* and elsewhere. A Canto Mundo fellow, she has also received scholarships/residencies from the Sundress Academy for the Arts, the Luso-American Development Foundation, and the Disquiet Literary Program. She is a member of the arts-activist groups Brick City Collective and Kale Soup for the Soul.

Ironically, while earning her MFA in creative writing at Rutgers, Newark, she rekindled her interest in visual art and is now a teaching artist-in-residence for the Glass Book Project, with artwork featured in several of its collections, as well as in exhibits at Index Art Center (Newark) and West Orange (NJ) Arts Council. She also continues to teach writing for various university programs.

She has been an un-famous soccer player, freestyle karate/kickboxing black belt, and road tripper. Her interests range from acting to understanding the greed underlying America's affordable housing and health insurance crises. She is ruminating somewhere as we speak.

For more info visit paulaneves.net or @itinerantmuse.

www.ingramcontent.com/pod-product-compliance
Lightning Source LLC
LaVergne TN
LVHW041510070426
835507LV00012B/1463